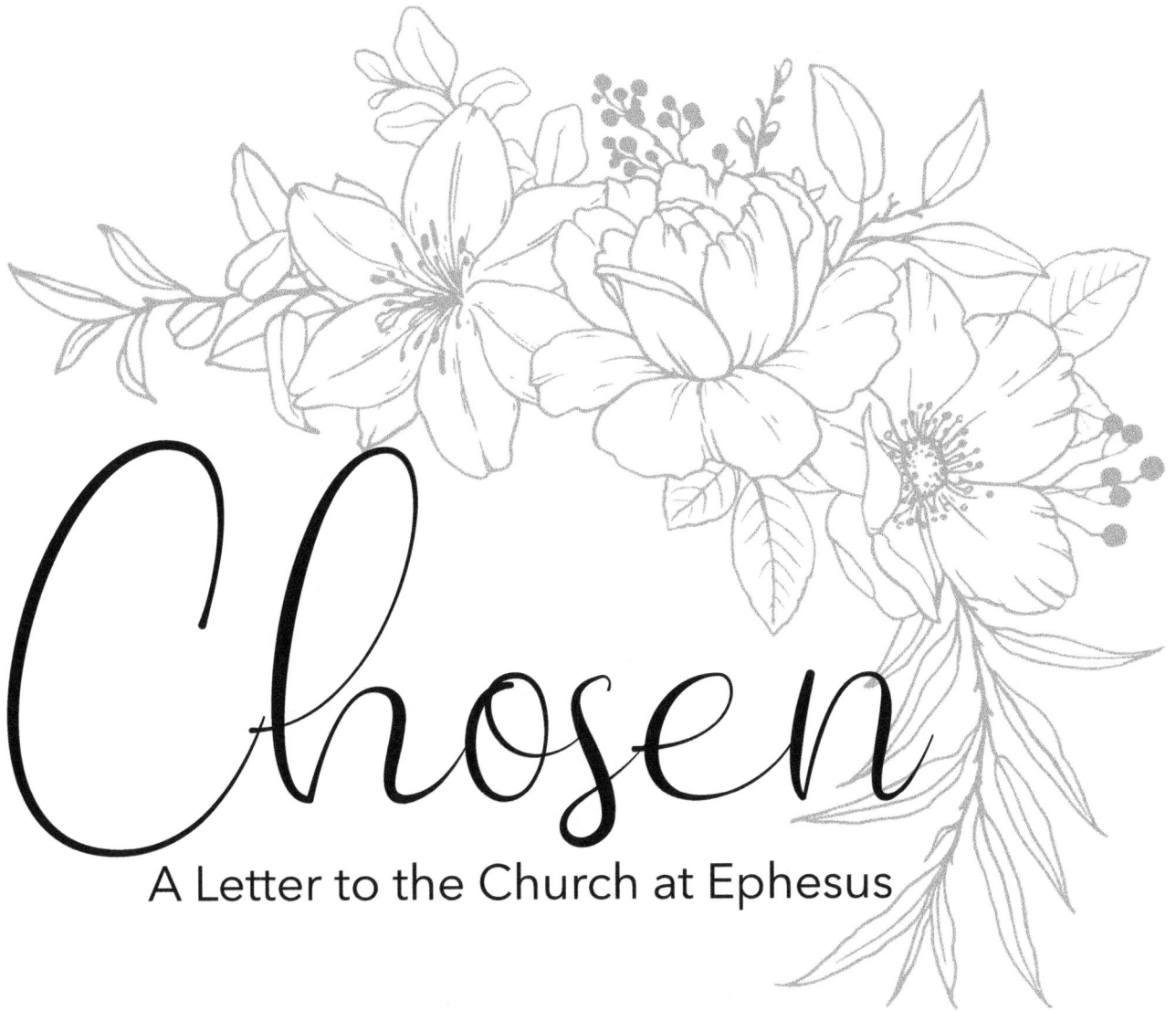

Chosen

A Letter to the Church at Ephesus

Written By Kim Day

Cover and illustration by Jill Reed Designs

Small group questions by Renee Westrope

A NOTE FROM KIM

Dear Fellow Student,

I am so glad that you have chosen to take this journey with me through the book of Ephesians. Our journey will not always be easy, but it will be profitable. I often tell a story about my family rock climbing in the mountains of Montana. I stayed below them on a narrow path and watched as they would grasp for hand and toe holds and inch their way up on a rock face. Their path wasn't easy, and their bodies testified to it as they had scrapes and bruises from the climb. But, as they reached the top that was ultimately out of my sight, I could hear them cheering. When they came down and we were reunited, they told me of all the things they saw from the top. The views were breathtaking! I had remained safe on the little path, so I could only imagine the things they spoke of because I did not do the climb.

This bible study is a little like taking the climb. Not every step will be easy; many of the things Paul writes to the Ephesians might be hard to understand and possibly something you might wrestle with. But, will it be worth it? It will be! Time in God's word is always worth it. I, too, am wrestling with some of the things written down, and I surely don't understand them all! I ask you to come to this study along with me, with open minds and hearts to understand and learn and with open palms to receive all that God has for us as we study this rich book, written as a letter to those who were believers in Ephesians.

Your fellow sojourner on the journey,

Kim Day

BIBLE STUDY TOOLS

The Bible is about God and His redemptive story. God created man and woman in His image and made us for a relationship with Him and with one another (Created state). Sin entered the human condition as man and woman doubted God and His word and chosing rebellion over obedience (Fallen state). Being full of mercy and justice, God made a way to restore this boken relationship allowing Him to dwell with sin-soaked men and women through sacrifice. This sacrifice started in the garden, and we see it through the pages of scripture until we see the complete sacrifice made through God's Son, Jesus Christ, on man and woman's behalf. Jesus satisfied once and for all God's requirements as He was the perfect sacrifice. Christ's sacrifice redeemed us from the fall and purchased us for God. (Redeemed state) This is the narrative of scripture. The over-arching story of all stories we find in the pages of scripture. We study the Bible to know Him, understand who He is, how He acts, and how then we shall live because He has chosen us.

In this study, we will be using observing, interpreting, and applying of scripture. We do that through asking questions, letting scripture speak for itself, and looking at resources. It is also essential that we study in that order. To jump to application before observing and interpreting can cause us to miss vital truths or adopt faulty meanings.

OBSERVATION	INTERPRETATION	APPLICATION
What Does it Say?	What Does it Mean?	What Does it Mean to Me?
Who wrote it?	Look at other scriptures that are about the same thing (cross-referencing)	How do we see God and the gospel?
To Whom was it written?		
Why was it written?	Look up words	How is God inviting me to live out this scripture?
What is going on?	Keep it in context	
When was it written?		What difference should it make to my daily life?
Historical context?		
What are the keywords and or themes?		

Feel free to look at commentaries and study notes in bibles **AFTER** doing your own work. You can use this method without a study. Pray and ask God to lead you and show you all that He wants you to see, and then just pick up your bible and some paper and a pen and study!

Resources For Study

With these resources, you will be able to look up words written in Hebrew and Greek lexicons. You will also be able to look at commentaries, cross reference, and parallel versions of scripture, which is often helpful when studying. These resources are free; other resources online are downloadable software.

https://www.biblestudytools.com/library/   https://www.blueletterbible.org/study.cfm

https://www.biblegateway.com/resources/dictionaries/   https://www.studylight.org/commentaries/

Kim's weekly teachings were recorded and a link to them can be found on her website at **KimDay.online**. Week one's homework will be the introduction and overview teaching on pages 8-9 of your study.

Chosen

A Letter to the Church at Ephesus

WEEK ONE

WEEK  ONE

Introduction and Overview
Weekly teaching can be found at KimDay.online.

Who wrote the Book of Ephesians?

When was it written?

To whom was it written?

What is the historical background?

What was the culture of Ephesus?

In what style is it written?

Where was it written?

What are the themes of the book of Ephesians?

What is the structure of the book?

Chapter 1:1-2, What do we learn?

PAUL'S MISSIONARY JOURNEYS

47-48 | First missionary journey with Barnabas to Cyprus and Galatia.

49-52 | Second missionary journey with Silas, through Asia Minor and Greece, settles in Corinth and writes to the Thessalonians.

52 | Begins Third Missionary journey. Stays in Ephesus. Writes to Galatians and Corinthians.

TIMELINE
PAUL'S RELATIONSHIP WITH THE EPHESIANS

Paul leaves Cornith and sails to Ephesus. Takes Pricilla and Aquilla. Church plant is started Acts 18:18--21
AD 52

**After a short visit the first time to Ephesus it is historcally believed that Paul spent over two years in Ephesus establishing and growing the church.

AD 54
Paul finds disciples of John the Baptist. Paul declares the gospel. Miracles happened. Acts 19:1-12

AD 56
Paul Leaves Ephesus and goes to Jerusalem. Acts 19:21

PAUL'S IMPRISONMENTS

57-59 | Returns to Jerusalem and arrested. Imprisoned at Caesarea.

59-60 | Appears before Festus and appeals to Caesar, voyage to Rome.

60-62 | Under house arrest at Rome. Writes letters to Philippians, Ephesians, Colossians, and Philemon.

62-64 | Released, journeys possibly to Spain. Writes letters to Timothy and Titus.

68 | Returns to Rome, imprisoned and martyred.

Paul sends for and says their
goodbyes to Ephesian Elders.
Arrested afterward.
Acts 20:17-38
AD 57

Paul urges Timothy to stay
at Ephesus to continue the work.
1 Timothy 1:3
AD 62

AD 60
Paul writes the letter to Ephesians
while imprisoned. Also writes
Colossians, Philippians,
and Philemon.

AD 67-68
Paul's final house arrest.
Acts 28:16, 30-31
It is also believed to
be Paul's death.

11

SESSION ONE **NOTES**

You can use the space below to take notes during the large group teaching session

SESSION ONE **NOTES**

Chosen

A Letter to the Church at Ephesus

WEEK TWO

WEEK TWO

1. Take a few moments to pray. Ask the Spirit of God to lead you into all truth as you begin to study this very rich book of Ephesians. (John 16:13)

Remember, what we call the book of Ephesians is a letter. Paul wrote a letter to the believing Christians in the churches at Ephesus. He planted the churches with the help of other faithful servants of God. Think about what it would have been like for them to receive a letter from Paul. They likely hung on every word written, being excited to hear from him and learn of his well-being. Ask God to let you approach this letter like that.

2. Read the entire letter from start to finish. It should take you about 20 minutes. If you are able, try to read it out loud. You have been provided a copy of the letter in the back of the study to read, mark, and write in the margins.

After reading, answer the following questions.

3. What stood out to you?

4. What questions did the reading prompt you to ask? Record them.
(While I'm reading a text, I often will just put a question mark (?) over something that I want to study more thoroughly)

5. If you have the time, re-read the letter noting specifically the questions above. We will start our deep dive tomorrow!

WEEK TWO

DAY TWO

Start with prayer over your time in God's word.

6. Read chapter one. Mark keywords and phrases in a manner that stands out to you. Make a note of any lists. Place a (?) over anything you question or want to study further.

7. Re-read 1:3-14

Paul begins by reminding the Ephesians of who they are **IN CHRIS**T and what has been given to them because of Christ! This is exciting stuff!

8. List identifying words for a person who is **IN CHRIST**. Underline each word in the same color. (I used green).

My list includes 9 identifying words that are true according to the word of God for a person who is IN CHRIST. (your list could be more or less)   Let's explore some of them.

Two of them are very close in meaning, CHOSEN and ADOPTED.

9. Write out definitions for each word.

Chosen:

Adopted:

17

APPLY:

10. What does it mean to you that you have been Chosen? Adopted?

11. What is the fact that you are Chosen based upon? (When answering questions like this one, try to use the words out of the scriptures. It will help sink them into your mind and heart.)

12. Another word on our list is PREDESTINED. Look this word up and write a definition.

13. Let's look at a few other scriptures that can give us a broader understanding of this word. Look up each reference and record what you learn about being predestined.

Romans 8:28-30

John 15:16

2 Timothy 1:9

Jeremiah 1:5

1 John 4:19

Even if we think back to when God saved the Israelites out of Egypt, He did so for them to be His people and for Him to be their God, and that others would know Him as the one true God. He did not choose them because of who they were but because of who He is. He chose them because He chose them. He loved them because He loved them. HE IS GOD. God uses "chose" and "chosen" repeatedly through scripture. It's because He is the initiator of relationship, and we are the responders. This truth should cause us to lean more deeply into the God who chooses!

14. Look up the word **IDENTITY** and record your definition.

15. Is the list we have made a definition of **IDENTITY**? Explain your answer.

16. What Identifying word is most precious to you? What identifying word do you want to explore more or gain more understanding about?

17. End today's study with a prayer of thanksgiving that God has chosen you! Even if you don't fully know what that means, I believe we will be exploring the knowledge that we are "chosen" until we draw our last breath!

18. Re-read Ephesians 1: 3-14, circle every time "In Him" or "In Christ" is mentioned.

Yesterday we made a list of identities based on Paul's writing. It is our identity because we are **IN CHRIST**.

19. Make a list of what an **IN CHRIST** person has been given. As you did yesterday with the identifying words, underline these words or phrases with the same color. (I used red)

APPLY
20. What does it mean that these things have been given to you because of Jesus? Write your response out to the Lord.

21. The phrase In Christ, or In Him could be stated this way: Because of Christ's completed work on your behalf, you have_____. What is Christ's completed work? Write it below.

22. Verse 13 says that those who believe in Him are "sealed with the promised Holy Spirit."

Look up the following verses and answer the questions.

Who promised the Holy Spirit?
What is the Holy Spirit's role in a believer's life?

John 14:15-17

John 16:15-21

23. Look up these verses about being sealed with the Spirit and record what you learn.

2 Corinthians 5:5

2 Corinthians 1:21-22

Ephesians 4:30

24. God placing His seal on His children through the Holy Spirit is to be a security for us. Do you look at it like that? Why or why not?

We will look at Paul's prayer for the Ephesian believers for the next two days.

25. Read Chapter 1:16-23

26. Paul begins this paragraph with "For this reason". What is Paul referring to as he begins this way?

27. What had Paul heard about them?

28. As Paul prays for them, what does he ask God for on their behalf?
List them below and mark his requests with a specific color on your copy of the letter.

29. The first thing Paul asked was that the Spirit of wisdom and revelation be given to them. That was sunk in what or whom? And does that matter?

APPLY

30. In whom or in what are you prone to sink your wisdom and or revelation in? Why is this dangerous? Explain your answer.

31. In the list of things Paul prayed, what catches your attention the most? What would you like to explore more? Do it!

32. The last thing Paul prays is that they may know the "immeasurable greatness of his power toward us who believe." He states that God has demonstrated this power. Through whom did God demonstrate His power? And How?

33. Where is Christ?

34. What has Christ been put above?

35. Is anything lacking in the list above?

36. What position does Christ hold? Who put Him there?

37. Who is the church?

APPLY

38. When you think of the church, what or who do you think about? How does the thought that Jesus is the head of the church deepen or change your thinking?

REFLECTION

Take a few minutes to pray that God will enlighten your eyes. Read through the five days of homework (both questions and answers). Then, answer the below questions.

What stood out to you this week?

How did you see God? (Father God, Jesus, and or the Holy Spirit)

How did you see the gospel?

What did God speak to you this week that challenged you or caused growth?

Is there anything you need to change or get help with to be obedient to what God has said?

SESSION TWO NOTES

You can use the space below to take notes during the large group teaching session

SMALL GROUP DISCUSSION

Week Two: Ephesians 1:3-23

Vs. 3-14: From the list you made of identifying words for those in Christ, which descriptions or characteristics stood out to you most? Why?

Vs. 4: Why is it sometimes difficult for us to remember and believe that we are chosen?

Vs. 5: What implications are there in the truth that we are adopted by the Father?

Vs. 13: How important is it that believers understand that we are sealed? What challenges or vulnerabilities can arise if we don't understand or believe this truth?

Vs 17: Why do you think Paul's request that believers be given "a spirit of wisdom and of revelation in the knowledge of him" is his foremost concern in this prayer?
   *Who or what is a danger for you to sink your wisdom and revelation in?

Vs. 18: Why do you think we have such a tendency to misunderstand and miss out of the riches we have in Christ? What things keep us from opening up our hearts to all God has given us?

Vs. 20-23: How should this truth that Christ is exalted above all alter the way you live every day life?

Chosen

A Letter to the Church at Ephesus

WEEK THREE

WEEK THREE

Remember, this "book" as we call it is, in actuality, a letter. A letter circulated to the churches of Ephesus to read. It continues to be circulated as we have picked it up to read and glean all God has for us! It is an excellent thought to consider how many people, our brothers and sisters from the past and those that will be family in the future, will read this same letter. This week, we will contemplate what it means to be part of the household of faith. Pray as you begin today, ask what He has for you to discover from His word.

1. Take 20 minutes and read the letter of Ephesians in its entirety.

2. Re-read chapter 2.

3. Mark any words or phrases that stick out to you. Make a note of any lists that you see. Place a (?) over anything you question or want to study more.

4. Summarize chapter two with 2-3 sentences.

5. Note anything in the chapter that you have a question about or want to explore further.

6. Read Chapter 2:1-10

7. Remember, in Paul's opening paragraphs in this letter, Paul reminds the Ephesians of what Jesus had secured for them and where thier identity lies - **IN CHRIST**. Now, Paul reminds them (and us) what our identity was before Christ. Using verses 1-3, make a list of who we were apart from Christ.

8. Verse 4's first two words might be the two most impactful words in the Bible. What are they?

_____   _____

9. How is God described in verse 4?

10. Write a prayer to God reflecting what verse 4 means to you.

11. Even when you were "dead" in your sin as the person that verses 1-3 described, God set His love on you through Christ Jesus and made you what?

12. Verse 6 describes what we call the "all ready not yet ." We are walking around in a broken world, still battling our sin and the sin around us, yet there is a future reality not yet experienced. Paul reminds the Ephesian believers of their position in Christ. Positionally where are we if we are **IN CHRIST**?

13. What is God's ongoing action towards those in Christ Jesus?

Apply:
14. Write how you experience the tension of being positionally seated with Christ, eternity settled, and the walking daily in the "not yet"?

15. Read Ephesians 2: 1-10

16. Write out verses 8-9 in the space provided.

Using a dictionary or Greek lexicon, look up the following words and write out their definition.

17. Grace:

18. Saved:

19. Faith:

20. Boast:

21. Using the above definitions and your understanding of the rest of the words and phrases in verses 8-9, write the verses in your own words, amplifying the meanings as you understand them.

22. Read verse 10. We are God's what?

23. Look up the word workmanship and record what you find.

24. What were we created for?

Apply:
25. Ponder the thought that you are His workmanship and created for good works that He has prepared. Write out your thoughts and questions about these statements. This might be something you want to talk about with a friend or mentor.

26. Read Ephesians 2:11-22

27. Paul identifies that the Ephesians, being Gentiles were separated from Christ. What were the conditions that separated them?

28. Look at Genesis 17:1-14, and record what circumcision was for and what God established.

29. If not a Jew and not circumcised, how did the Ephesians (or anyone) become reconciled to God?

30. Christ became our _____. (vs. 14)

Apply
31. Jesus became our peace. He broke every barrier for all people and reconciled us to God through His blood. That blood purchased a new identity, new DNA if you will, making us a part of His family. Either using your name or the pronoun "I". Write verse 13 in your own words and express what this fact means to you.

32. Read Ephesians 2:11-22.

33. List the contrasting language used throughout these verses in list form. (hint: far <> near)

34. Christ reached across every barrier to reconcile us to God and make us a part of His family. Paul calls the Ephesians fellow citizens and members of the household of God. What imagery does he use?

35. Look up the following verses to get a broader scriptural view of what Paul is describing. Write under each what you discover.

Galatians 3:26-28

1 Peter 2:4-5

John 17:21-23

36. What foundation is the "household of faith" built on? (2:20) How important is a foundation to a house?

37. Who is the cornerstone? What role does a cornerstone play in a building? You might want to look it up and get a construction lesson!

38. This house, this structure built together, is the dwelling place for Whom?

39. Look up these verses and record what you learn.

John 14:17

1 Corinthians 6:19-20

Apply:
40. We often make our Christianity individualistic. Through Christ's completed work, it is true that God has saved us and is sanctifying us as individuals. It is also true that our Christianity was never meant to be only or wholly individualistic. We are a part of God's family, one living stone among many stones, one member among many members, and we are being put together and built as God's household. We are the church! How do you view yourself in relationship to the church?

REFLECTION

Take a few minutes to pray that God will enlighten your eyes. Read through the five days of homework (both questions and answers). Then answer the below questions.

What stood out to you this week?

How did you see God? (Father God, Jesus, and or the Holy Spirit)

How did you see the gospel?

What did God speak to you this week that challenged you or caused growth?

Is there anything you need to change or get help with to be obedient to what God has said?

SESSION THREE NOTES

You can use the space below to take notes during the large group teaching session

SESSION THREE NOTES

SMALL GROUP DISCUSSION

Week Three: Ephesians 2

Vs. 1-3: Does the phrase "dead in sin" and other descriptors in these verses accurately describe your experience before you became a Christian? How?

Vs. 5: What is so significant about the truth that God saved us at our worst?

Vs. 8-9: Why is this passage so important for believers to really understand and accept?

Vs. 10: What things can hinder us from walking in the good works that "God prepared beforehand".

Vs. 10: What practical things can we do to walk in the truth that we are His workmanship, created for good works?

Vs. 14: What areas in your life do you need to understand and experience more fully that "He himself is our peace…"?

Vs. 19-21: How do you view yourself in relationship to the church?

Vs. 14-21: We see that Christ broke down every barrier between us and God AND between each other. What barriers do we continue to battle against that contribute to disunity or division among our church body?

Vs. 19-22: What practical steps/actions/habits can we take to move towards unity?

Chosen

A Letter to the Church at Ephesus

WEEK FOUR

WEEK FOUR

We will focus our attention on chapter three of Ephesians this week. In this section of Paul's letter, he will continue to write theological content. It is theology that he believed the Ephesian church needed in order to be confident and live the life God had for them. We, too, need to know this theology to understand how to live as God's women, as a members of the church, and engage the world around us.

1. Read Chapters 1-3 of Ephesians

2. Re-read chapter 3.

3. Mark any words or phrases that stick out to you. Make a note of any lists you see. Place a (?) over anything you question or further study.

4. Summarize chapter three with 2-3 sentences.

5. Note anything in the chapter that you have a question about or want to explore more.

6. Read Ephesians 3:1-13

7. Paul identifies himself how?

8. On whose behalf?

9. What is Paul's condition according to verse 13?

10. Did Paul know that suffering was a part of the mission he was called to? Look at Acts 9:15-16 and record your answer.

11. Many Christians today promote a health and wealth gospel that tells them that we should never suffer if we are in Christ. Look at the following verses and record what you learn. Also, think through or look at the stories of men in the Bible other than Paul, (i.e.Job, Joseph, and David)..

2 Timothy 3:12

1 Peter 5:8-10

1 John 3:13

John 15:20

Apply:
12. Write your theological view on suffering.

13. Read Ephesians 3:1-13

14. Paul wrote several letters from prison. Read Colossians 1: 24-29, a parallel passage to the one we are studying. Record any insights that stick out to you.

15. Paul says he was made a minister of what?

16. How does he describe the gospel in this section?

Apply:
17. How would you describe the gospel? Write out the gospel in your own words.

18. Those of us who have been "brought near" through the gospel know the mystery that Paul speaks of. Do you share it? If someone asked you "what is the gospel?", what would you say? Take the sentences that you wrote above and practice speaking the gospel. I would encourage you to practice with someone else and then be so bold to ask God to allow you to share the gospel with someone this week!

19. Read Ephesian 3:14-21.

20. Again, Paul will let them in on how he is praying for them. What is his posture?

21. To Whom is he praying and why?

22. List the things that Paul is praying for them.

Let's answer a few questions to understand the list above.

23. Where does all of what he asks for them flow from?

24. Who strengthens us with power?

Apply:
25. What stands out to you about Paul's prayer?

26. Form Paul's prayer for the Ephesians as a prayer for yourself, those you love, and for God's church. Take the time today to pray these words. I would encourage you to think about your posture as well, and bend your knee.

27. Read Ephesians 3: 14-20.

28. According to verse 17, as Christ dwells in our hearts through faith, we are being rooted and grounded in love. Look up the following words to understand the word picture being painted.

Dwell:

Rooted:

Grounded:

29. What will we be able to comprehend if the above is taking place in our lives?

Apply:
30. Do you know that God loves you? Based upon the study of Ephesians to this point, how do you know God loves you?

31. What role does dwelling and being rooted and grounded play in us knowing God's love?

32. Re-read verse 20. It is as if Paul is putting a giant exclamation point on this section of his letter! How does it show our God?

33. Where is God's glory to be displayed?

R E F L E C T I O N

Take a few minutes to pray that God will enlighten your eyes, read through the five days of homework (questions and answers). Then answer the below questions.

What stood out to you this week?

How did you see God? (Father God, Jesus, and or the Holy Spirit)

How did you see the gospel?

What did God speak to you this week that challenged you or caused growth?

Is there anything you need to change or get help with to be obedient to what God has said?

SESSION FOUR NOTES

You can use the space below to take notes during the large group teaching session

SESSION FOUR NOTES

SMALL GROUP DISCUSSION

Week Four: Ephesians 3

Vs. 13: What thoughts did you have concerning your theological view on suffering? Why is this such a hard topic for us to grasp/accept?

Vs. 14-19: Reflect on the most consistent content of your prayers for the people in your life and also yourself. How does it compare to the things Paul prays for his brothers and sisters? What shifts need to be made?

Vs. 17: Practically, how does it look to be "rooted and grounded in love"?

Vs. 18: On day 5 of homework this week, we are asked the question, "how do you know God loves you?". What were some of your responses, and what kinds of things cause us to question or doubt His love for us?

Vs. 20: We are praying to a God who "is able to do far more abundantly than all that we ask or think…". How should this truth impact our prayer life and our faith?

Chosen

A Letter to the Church at Ephesus

WEEK FIVE

WEEK FIVE
DAY ONE

1. Read through the entire book of Ephesians.

Paul has laid a beautiful theological foundation for us in chapters 1-3. For the rest of his letter, he will address how to live out that theology practically. Paul exhorts the Ephesian church (and us) to maintain unity, use our gifts, and grow spiritually. We will focus our study this week on chapter four.

2. Read Ephesians 4:1-16, and mark keywords and phrases. Make a note of any lists. Place a (?) over anything you have questions or want to learn more about.

3. What is the first admonition given?

4. This is a repeated admonition in Paul's letters. Look up these other references and write what you believe he is talking about. Hint: Don't forget that Paul starts this paragraph of his letter with a "therefore."

Colossians 1:10

1 Thessalonians 2:9-16

Philippians 1:27

5. Verses 2-3 tell us how walking worthy looks. List what it looks like.

Apply
6. Ponder the list you made above. Are there any areas in your life in which you are not walking worthy? Where do you need to ask God to help you? Take the time to talk to the Lord about what needs to change.

7. Read Ephesians 4:1-16

8. Fill in the blanks

_____body   _____baptism

_____Spirit   _____God and Father

_____hope

_____Lord

_____faith

9. What is Paul trying to communicate by reminding them that there is only one of the above stated?

Paul writes Psalm 68:18 and then summarizes the psalm. The psalm is a victory hymn for a conquering King. Verses 9-10 function like parentheses, then he speaks of Christ's descent and ascent. Paul sees the incarnation of Christ (decent) and the ascension of Christ as evidence that Christ is Savior and King. Christ is our conquering King who is above all, fills all, and gives gifts to all.

10. Look back at verse 7. Grace here is not referring to saving grace but to something that is a gift given. Using the words as found in the verse, who has received this gift?

11. Does that leave anyone out?

12. These "gifts" given according to Christ's gift are spiritual gifts. Here in Ephesians, these gifts are appointed offices to the church. List them.

13. What is the specific reason these gifts are given according to the scripture?

14. If "each one" has been given a gift according to the measure of Christ's gift. Then that means you and I have one or more. Look at the following passages and record what you learn about spiritual gifts, please be mindful of why gifts are given, and what some of them are.

Romans 12:3-8

1 Corinthians 12 - 14

1 Peter 4:10-11

Apply:
15. Do you know your spiritual gifting? If you don't, look at the above passages and ask the Lord to reveal how He desires you to function in the body. You might want to talk this over with a friend or mentor. Please be mindful of why gifts were given. They have less to do about us (so we can't sink our identity into them) and more to do with our Christ!

16. Read Ephesians 4: 1-16

17. What would you say is the goal of gifts being given?

18. After the list of gifts given to the church to equip the saints, Paul talks about growth. List the varied words that are used as synonyms for the word growth.

19. We are to "no longer be children." What are some identifying marks of children according to these verses? Give an example of what each means.

Apply:

20. Do you see areas in your own life where you need growth as you consider the list above?

21. Growing up is not an individual event. How does Paul describe it?

22. Who is the head?

Apply:
23. The church is to function as a body. Just as our physical bodies have different parts that all work together, the church with many different parts is to work together in function, growth, and purpose. Just as the body isn't just a bunch of feet or eyes or hands, the church body is many different members joined together. Write how you have seen this play out in your own experience.

24. Maybe this is the first time you have thought about the church functioning as a body, and you are one part of it. Or maybe you have known this, but this study has allowed you to re-fresh this thought. Are you a functioning member of the body? Is there anything that needs to change for growth?

25. Read Ephesians 4: 17-32.

26. Paul again, as he did in verse 1 of chapter 4, refers to their walk. What is he referring to?

27. The Ephesians were Gentiles! Paul told them to no longer walk like they once did or like those around them. List what those around them were "walking" like.

28. Look up the word callous and record what you learn.

29. Becoming callous resulted in what?

Apply:
30. Have you ever become calloused? What did it result in your life?

Paul insists that they did not learn Christ in this manner or way! What was he referring to? I believe he was saying; that they did not learn that they could trust in Christ and become His followers and then live however they wanted and or continue in their old way of living.

He uses the terms "put off" and "put on" to visualize our old and new lives, likening it to clothing.

31. Read Colossians 3: 5-14, another "put off" and "put on" passage.

32. Combining what we see in Ephesians 4: 22-32 and Colossians 3:5-14, What are we to Put On and what are we to Put Off? Make a note of how that is accomplished if it is stated.

PUT OFF   **HOW**   **PUT ON**

33. Read Ephesians 4: 17-32

34. In verses 26 - 32, Paul gives many admonitions for daily living with one another. List them.

35. Many of these, even being angry, have to do with our words. Look at the following verses and record the importance of our words according to scripture.

Proverbs 11:9

Proverbs 11:12

Proverbs 11:17

Proverbs 15:1

Proverbs 15:4

Proverbs 16:24

Proverbs 18:20-21

Proverbs 25:18

36. How are we to handle anger?

37. If we don't handle our anger, to whom do we give an opportunity to?

38. If one is a thief, how are we to handle our stealing? And, for what purpose?

39. Look up the word corrupt and record what you learn.

40. If we are to let no corrupt talk come out of our mouths, what kind of words are to come out of our mouths?

By Paul's admonition to not grieve the Holy Spirit, we can assert that practicing the opposite of what Paul is saying does grieve the Holy Spirit that lives within us.

Apply:
41. What does it mean to grieve someone? Take time to think about grieving the Holy Spirit. Write out your thoughts.

42. Paul ends this paragraph with verse 32 as a giant exclamation point to this section. Write the verse out in the space given.

43. How could the practice of this verse avoid the grieving of the Holy Spirit?

R E F L E C T I O N

Take a few minutes to pray that God will enlighten your eyes, read through the five days of homework (questions and answers). Then answer the below questions.

What stood out to you this week?

How did you see God? (Father God, Jesus, and or the Holy Spirit)

How did you see the gospel?

What did God speak to you this week that challenged you or caused growth?

Is there anything you need to change or get help with to be obedient to what God has said?

SESSION FIVE NOTES

You can use the space below to take notes during the large group teaching session

SESSION FIVE **NOTES**

SMALL GROUP DISCUSSION

Week Five: Ephesians 4

Vs. 1: What obstacles can most often hinder us in our effort to "walk in a manner worthy" of our calling?

Vs . 4-6: In Day 2 of our homework, what thoughts did you have about what Paul was trying to communicate in emphasizing the "one-ness" of the things listed?

Vs. 11: On Day 2, we looked at several other passages on the various spiritual gifts. How can the existence of different spiritual gifts help bring about unity and growth in the body? How can differing gifts sometimes spark controversy or division?

Vs. 12: Why is it so important that we know and remember the purpose of God in his giving each of us spiritual gifts?

Vs. 15-16: How can we participate more fully in this process of growth within the context of our local church body?

Vs. 17-18: Thinking about our own culture and context, how would you describe how those that are lost "walk"?

Vs. 19: What practical things can we do to prevent becoming calloused to walking in some of those ways?

Vs. 22-32: We made a list in our homework on Day 4 of things to "put off" and things to "put on". What does this actually look like in our daily lives?

Vs. 25-32 There are many commands and exhortations in this short section. Which ones are most challenging to you personally?

Chosen

A Letter to the Church at Ephesus

WEEK SIX

WEEK ✿ SIX
DAY ONE

1. Read the entire letter (out loud if that helps you retain).

2. Re-read chapter 5:1 - 6:9. Mark keywords and phrases, make notes in the margin of anything that stands out to you, and put a (?) over anything you question or want to study further.

3. Summarize this passage of the letter in 3-4 sentences.

Remember that Ephesians is divided into two sections. The first half is theology, a reminder of who our God is and who we are because of Him. The second half is practical theology describing how we are to live out the truth about our God and ourselves in everyday life. The entire letter is written to the church. Our theology is not just lived on Sundays when the church meets, or it shouldn't be! Instead, our theology is lived out every day and within every relationship. A common question I ask myself is, "Does my reality match my theology?" I want you to ask yourself that question. We can know a lot about God, know the correct answers, and pretend to follow Him for a little while. Eventually, what transforms us or conforms us will be seen in our everyday lives. God and His gospel change us as whole people, and the power of the gospel and the transformation of our entire lives then plays itself out in our everyday moments and relationships. Paul will take his admonitions to even deeper levels of relationships this week and apply them to the closest daily relationships, husbands and wives, parents and children, and employers and employees.

Apply:
As you end your time today, would you take a few more moments and ask yourself the question I asked above and answer in the space provided.

4. Does your reality match your theology?

5. Read Ephesians 5:1-21.

6. This section of Paul's letter starts with a "therefore." Therefore always refers back to a previous thought. Go back and refresh your thinking about what Paul was writing before he began this section of his letter and what he said in these 21 verses. What is the referencing with his "therefore"?

7. Be imitators of Whom?

8. Look up the word Imitator and write a definition. What does it mean for you to imitate God?

9. How are you to imitate God? As what? _____.

10. How did you become beloved children? Has that already been answered in Paul's letter? Write out how that took place for the Ephesians and you!

11. List what should not be "named among us." Take the time to look up the words on this list that you need to understand. For example, do you know what crude joking means? Remember, you have access to Greek lexicons on the links provided on the resource page. This will give you the meaning Paul thought when he wrote. Or, look them up in a dictionary.

There are some qualifying phrases attached to this list of actions and behaviors. They stick out to me, and I want you to notice them.

"not named among you" v. 3
"proper among saints" v. 3
"out of place" v. 4
"try to discern what is pleasing to the Lord" v. 10

Apply:
12. What are your thoughts about the list you made and Paul's admonitions in the phrases I wrote above? Possibly you have blurred the line between what the word has to say and what culture says or what is comfortable for you. Write a response to what you believe the Lord is saying to you.

13. Read Ephesians 5:1-21

Paul makes a series of contrasts in this section to bring understanding to his readers. Let's explore them.

Example of contrast:
>"let no filthiness, nor foolish talk, nor crude joking" be a part of how you talk
<"but instead let there be thanksgiving" "addressing one another in psalms and hymns and spiritual songs."

Write out what you learn from the other two contrasts found in this section. Take the time to dig for yourself, cross-reference, and find other scriptures on the subject.

14. Darkness <> Light

15. Unwise <> Wise

Paul ends this paragraph with two last admonitions that I believe are spiritual keys in our lives. Let's look at them.

16. Write out verse 20.

17. How often are you to give thanks?

18. For what are you to give thanks?

19. To Whom are you to give thanks?

20. What is the opposite of giving thanks?

Apply:
Elizabeth Elliot is someone that I call a mentor-from-afar. She has encouraged, challenged, and inspired me in my walk with Christ. She says, "It is always possible to be thankful for what is given rather than resentful over what is withheld. One attitude or the other becomes a way of life." What is your attitude?

21. Write out verse 21

22. Look up the word submit and write out a definition.

23. Who are we to submit to?

24. Out of what is our submission to flow?

The word here is not referring to one being superior and one being subservient. Submission is a biblical word used in how we treat one another within the church.

There are many verses in the New Testament that we call the "one another's" of scripture. They tell us how we are to treat one another. Look at these verses and see if they give you an expanded understanding. Write what you learn and how being submitted to one another plays out within them.

Romans 12:10

Romans 12:16

1 Thessalonians 5: 11, 15

Galatians 5:26

WEEK SIX

Before you begin today, you need to remember the context of Paul's letter. To whom it is written and the purposes we have already seen are pivotal as we move forward. The passage we will be looking at today is what most people consider a marriage passage. It is not a marriage passage; it is a church passage (5:32). Paul uses marriage as a living picture of an intimate and unbreakable relationship. That being said, we can learn much about God-centered marriage from this passage! I don't believe we can read verses 22-33 without being reminded of verses 18-21 of chapter 5. God-centered relationships flow out of being filled with the Spirit!

26. Read Ephesians 5:18-33

27. What are we to be filled with?

28. As a result, list what flows out of that?

Now we are ready to look at 22-33. Apart from the Spirit's control and work, we will always fight this passage.

29. What is the response of a wife within marriage? If needed, refresh yourself from yesterday's homework.

30. How is this to be done?

31. What is the response of a husband within marriage?

32. Why is this to be done?

33. Read Genesis 2:15-25
34. Who created and instituted marriage?

35. Who gets to say what it looks like?

Based on our passage today and with the Genesis passage;
36. What is the ultimate picture of marriage?

37. What is the ultimate purpose of marriage?

Apply:
38. Has the study of this passage today created questions? Or, if you are married, has it shown areas in your marriage that need the Spirit's work? Do you need help in your marriage? There are people who are willing to walk alongside you and your husband! Write out your answers and a prayer of what you would like to see God do in your marriage or marriages around you.

WEEK ❀ SIX
DAY FIVE

We are not stopping at chapter 5 because the first of Chapter 6 continues with two primary relationships where our theology plays out. Remember that God-centered relationships flow out of being filled with the Spirit

39. Read Ephesians 6:1-4

40. What are children's responses to be?

41. Paul cites that this is the first commandment with promise. What commandment is he referring to? (Look at Exodus 20:1-17) Write out the commandment.

42. Look up the word Honor and write a definition.

43. What are parents' roles and responses?

44. Write out what you believe it means to provoke your child to anger.

45. Write out what you believe it looks like to bring up children in the discipline and instruction of the Lord.

Context: Where we can apply these few verses to employees and employers I don't want us to jump there too quickly because we might miss some of what Paul is instructing. It also would be a mistake for us to apply our American context of slavery to this passage. Paul has been speaking to the household of faith and then narrows the lens as he brings it into the family household. We have looked at the marriage relationship and the parent/child relationship. It would stand reasonable to look at the slave/master relationship because most homes would have this as a part of daily life within the home. The situation Paul addresses with slaves and masters was not like slavery in American history. It was complex and massive in scope. American slavery was primarily racial and lifelong. When and where Paul was writing from, slavery was not racial, and it was not always lifelong.

In most cases, it was a way of provision, a form of paying debt, and a method of employment. It was accepted as part of the Mediterranean world's economic life. I know from where we sit; it is a diabolical thought. Let's take these verses at face value and see what God says to us from them.

46. Read 6:5-9

47. What was to be the response of the bondslave?

48. How are they to do this?

Earlier in our homework, we established that all relationships can only be God-centered if they flow out of being Spirit-filled. Submission is always a reflection of our heart toward God.

49. Paul's admonition was that they were not to serve by eye service. If they did, they would be what?

50. What was to be the response of the master?

51. Why? What does Paul want the masters to be mindful of?

52. What do you see about God?

Apply:
In each section of the letter, husband and wives, parents and children, and bondservants and masters, there are the phrases; "as to the Lord," "in the Lord," "as you would Christ." What does this communicate to you about our motivation in relationships?

REFLECTION

Take a few minutes to pray that God will enlighten your eyes, read through the five days (questions and answers). Then answer the below questions.

What stood out to you this week?

How did you see God? (Father God, Jesus, and or the Holy Spirit)

How did you see the gospel?

What did God speak to you this week that challenged you or caused growth?

Is there anything you need to change or get help with to be obedient to what God has said?

SESSION SIX NOTES

You can use the space below to take notes during the large group teaching session

SESSION SIX **NOTES**

SMALL GROUP DISCUSSION

Week Six: Ephesians 5 – 6:1-9

Vs. 1: What does it mean to be imitators of God?

Vs. 3-5: Paul is pushing back firmly against behaviors that surely were commonplace and accepted in the current culture. Do you find these admonitions to believers in our culture today to still be necessary or relevant? How so, or why not?

Vs. 7-13: Why is the darkness/light contrast such a repeated and powerful metaphor throughout Scripture?

Vs. 20: Reread Elizabeth Elliot's quote from Day 3 of your homework. How can we battle against the attitudes of resentment or ingratitude?

Vs. 21: On Day 3, we looked up several verses on submission. How does our culture define submission?

What challenged you most from the verses we looked up about how we can and should live in submission to one another in the Body?

Vs. 22: How can those truths about submitting to one another help us understand the next verse commanding wives to submit to your husbands?

6:1: What do we, as adults, do with Paul's command to children? Does the call to honor our parents remain with us and if so, how is that supposed to look?

Chosen

A Letter to the Church at Ephesus

WEEK SEVEN

WEEK SEVEN

This is our last week of homework! Can you believe it? I pray this rich book has been used in the Spirit's care, and while you have presented yourself as a workman handling God's word accurately, it has transformed your life! I'm praying for you as you enter into the final sentences of Paul's letter.

This final section is about the Armor of God. God has always provided clothing for His children. After sin entered into the human condition, God killed an animal and provided clothing to cover Adam and Eve's nakedness. As the Israelites wandered in the wilderness, God didn't let their clothes wear out so they could know His provision through what they wore. When we get to peek into the heavenly realms in Revelation, we see that we will be clothed in white robes that will be provided for us. In other places in scripture, we see that there is spiritual clothing that we are to put on if we are in Christ.

1.Look up these verses and list the spiritual clothing we should be wearing as God's people.

Colossians 3:12

Isaiah 61:10

2. Read Ephesians 6: 10-24. Mark keywords and phrases. Make notes in the margin and place (?'s) over anything you question or want to study further.

3. What is Paul's first admonition in this section?

4. What is Paul's instruction about the armor of God?

5. What does that tell you?

Apply:
6. This section of scripture shows us areas in which we need to participate with God for growth and life. Paul says that we need to "put on" this spiritual clothing. It is not a passive or a casual admonition. He is saying, "Do this!" Do we believe that God's word and transformational change will jump on us somehow? Are we passive and casual about the commands and admonitions in scripture? That's like knowing that a load of laundry needs to be done and hoping it gets done. Does that work? No, I will have to get up, put it in the washing machine, place the clothes in the dryer, and fold and put the clothes away for the load of laundry to be considered "finished." You have been studying for six weeks, so I know you have participated. This is an excellent time to ask, what will your participation look like after this bible study is over? How do you plan on continuing to participate with God in your transformation and growth?

7. Read Ephesians 6:10-24

8. "Put on the whole armor of God that you may be able to _____ against the _____ of the devil."

9. What does it mean to stand? It's mentioned four times! What is the opposite of standing?

10. Look up the word schemes in a Greek lexicon and record what you find.

11. Rewrite verses 10-11 in your own words and based on the definitions you found.

12. Who do we NOT wrestle against? And, what does that mean? (make it personal)

13. Who we do wrestle against.

14. Take the time to look up this passage in different Bible translations (NAS, NIV). Look in a paraphrase like the application bible or message and record anything you learn from this exercise.

Apply:
15. Do you believe spiritual warfare is real? Have you experienced warfare or the wrestle that Paul describes? Were you able to stand? If yes, how (based upon our scripture, there is a correct answer)? If not, what are you learning that you know you will put into practice?

16. Our faithful and providing God, as He always does, gives us some spiritual clothing for the war and wrestling in which we are engaged. List each article of clothing and write out what each is to be used for. If it isn't clearly described, write what you believe is the usage for the particular article.

A.

B.

C.

D.

E.

F.

17. For fun, color this picture of the armor of God and label each article.

18. Read Ephesians 6:10-24.

19. How often and how are we to pray?

20. Are prayer and supplication different? Look up the words and record what you learn.

21. Paul tells them to "keep alert with all perseverance." What does that look like, and how can that translate into your daily life?

22. Paul closes his letter by asking them to pray for him. List his prayer requests.

23. Paul once again gives a picture of where he is and how he views himself. What are those two things?

24. How was Paul living his ambassadorship out even in prison? (hint: we are the benefactors of it!)

Paul's final words to them express his care for them and knowledge that they care for him. He was sending Tychicus with the letter.

25. How is Tychicus described?

26. What will he convey that is not in the letter?

27. What is another purpose for Paul sending Tychicus?

28. Paul closes his letter the way he started it, with peace and grace. Write out Paul's final sentences of this remarkable letter. Verses 23-24

29. Do you hear any final words that Paul wants to be deposited in the Ephesian believers? It's almost like when my teenagers would grab the keys to go somewhere, and I would follow them out the door, telling them everything I wanted them to know. To whom are his final words addressed?

We made it! If you have made it this far, well done! I pray the study of this section of scripture will be hidden in your heart and affect you for the rest of your life. It has been a pure joy to journey with you.

30. One last time, curl up in a chair, get a cup of tea or coffee, and read the letter of Ephesians out loud if possible. Read it with all the insight God has given you over the past seven weeks!

31. Take the time today to write out the things that God spoke to you, the things He challenged you with, and the things you are taking with you due to your study in the letter to the Ephesians and your study.

REFLECTION

Take a few minutes to pray that God will enlighten your eyes, read through the five days of homework and your answers, then answer the below questions.

What stood out to you this week?

How did you see God? (Father God, Jesus, and or the Holy Spirit)

How did you see the gospel?

What did God speak to you this week that challenged you or caused growth?

Is there anything you need to change or get help with to be obedient to what God has said?

SESSION SEVEN **NOTES**

You can use the space below to take notes during the large group teaching session

SESSION SEVEN NOTES

SMALL GROUP DISCUSSION

Week Seven: Ephesians 6:10-24

Vs 10-18: What verbs do we see commanded that reinforce the truth that we are responsible to participate in this work of God's transformation and spiritual battle?

Vs. 11-12: What does Paul mean when he states "we do not wrestle against flesh and blood"? Without eternal, spiritual perspective, what can we instead believe we are wrestling against when we face life struggles?

Vs. 13: Share a personal example of a time you experienced warfare and what practical things you did to stand against it.

Vs. 18: Paul tells us to "keep alert". What practical ways could we increase our awareness of the spiritual conflict going on around us?

Vs. 18: What hinders us from this kind of prayer life? What have you found helpful in developing consistency in your own prayer habits?

Ephesians

1 1 Paul, an apostle of Christ Jesus by the will of God, To the saints who are in Ephesus, and are faithful in Christ Jesus: 2 Grace to you and peace from God our Father and the Lord Jesus Christ. 3 Blessed be the God and Father of our Lord Jesus Christ, who has blessed us in Christ with every spiritual blessing in the heavenly places, 4 even as he chose us in him before the foundation of the world, that we should be holy and blameless before him. In love 5 he pre-destined us for adoption to himself as sons through Jesus Christ, according to the purpose of his will, 6 to the praise of his glorious grace, with which he has blessed us in the Beloved. 7 In him we have redemption through his blood, the forgiveness of our trespasses, according to the riches of his grace, 8 which he lavished upon us, in all wisdom and insight 9 making known to us the mystery of his will, according to his purpose, which he set forth in Christ 10 as a plan for the fullness of time, to unite all things in him, things in heaven and things on earth.

11 In him we have obtained an inheritance, having been predestined according to the purpose of him who works all things according to the counsel of his will, 12 so that we who were the first to hope in Christ might be to the praise of his glory. 13 In him you also, when you heard the word of truth, the gospel of your salvation, and believed in him, were sealed with the promised Holy Spirit, 14 who is the guarantee of our inheritance until we acquire possession of it, to the praise of his glory. 15 For this reason, because I have heard of your faith in the Lord Jesus and your love toward all the saints,

16 I do not cease to give thanks for you, remembering you in my prayers, 17 that the God of our Lord Jesus Christ, the Father of glory, may give you the Spirit of wisdom and of revelation in the knowledge of him, 18 having the eyes of your hearts enlightened, that you may know what is the hope to which he has called you, what are the riches of his glorious inheritance in the saints, 19 and what is the immeasurable greatness of his power toward us who believe, according to the working of his great might 20 that he worked in Christ when he raised him from the dead and seated him at his right hand in the heavenly places, 21 far above all rule and authority and power and dominion, and above every name that is named, not only in this age but also in the one to come. 22 And he put all things under his feet and gave him as head over all things to the church, 23 which is his body, the fullness of him who fills all in all.

2 And you were dead in the trespasses and sins 2 in which you once walked, following the course of this world, following the prince of the power of the air, the spirit that is now at work in the sons of disobedience— 3 among whom we all once lived in the passions of our flesh, carrying out the desires of the body and the mind, and were by nature children of wrath, like the rest of mankind. 4 But God, being rich in mercy, because of the great love with which he loved us, 5 even when we were dead in our trespasses, made us alive together with Christ—by grace you have been saved— 6 and raised us up with him and seated us with him in the heavenly places in Christ Jesus, 7 so that in the coming ages he might show the immeasurable riches of his grace in kindness toward us in Christ Jesus. 8 For by grace you have been saved through faith. And this is not your own doing; it is the gift of God, 9 not a result of works, so that no one may boast.

10 For we are his workmanship, created in Christ Jesus for good works, which God prepared beforehand, that we should walk in them.

11 Therefore remember that at one time you Gentiles in the flesh, called "the uncircumcision" by what is called the circumcision, which is made in the flesh by hands— 12 remember that you were at that time separated from Christ, alienated from the commonwealth of Israel and strangers to the covenants of promise, having no hope and without God in the world. 13 But now in Christ Jesus you who once were far off have been brought near by the blood of Christ. 14 For he himself is our peace, who has made us both one and has broken down in his flesh the dividing wall of hostility 15 by abolishing the law of commandments expressed in ordinances, that he might create in himself one new man in place of the two, so making peace, 16 and might reconcile us both to God in one body through the cross, thereby killing the hostility. 17 And he came and preached peace to you who were far off and peace to those who were near. 18 For through him we both have access in one Spirit to the Father. 19 So then you are no longer strangers and aliens, but you are fellow citizens with the saints and members of the household of God, 20 built on the foundation of the apostles and prophets, Christ Jesus himself being the cornerstone, 21 in whom the whole structure, being joined together, grows into a holy temple in the Lord. 22 In him you also are being built together into a dwelling place for God by the Spirit.

3 For this reason I, Paul, a prisoner of Christ Jesus on behalf of you Gentiles— 2 assuming that you have heard of the stewardship of God's grace that was given to me for you,

3 how the mystery was made known to me by revelation, as I have written briefly. 4 When you read this, you can perceive my insight into the mystery of Christ,

5 which was not made known to the sons of men in other generations as it has now been revealed to his holy apostles and prophets by the Spirit. 6 This mystery is that the Gentiles are fellow heirs, members of the same body, and partakers of the promise in Christ Jesus through the gospel.

7 Of this gospel I was made a minister according to the gift of God's grace, which was given me by the working of his power. 8 To me, though I am the very least of all the saints, this grace was given, to preach to the Gentiles the unsearchable riches of Christ, 9 and to bring to light for everyone what is the plan of the mystery hidden for ages in God, who created all things,

10 so that through the church the manifold wisdom of God might now be made known to the rulers and authorities in the heavenly places. 11 This was according to the eternal purpose that he has realized in Christ Jesus our Lord, 12 in whom we have boldness and access with con-fidence through our faith in him. 13 So I ask you not to lose heart over what I am suffering for you, which is your glory.

14 For this reason I bow my knees before the Father, 15 from whom every family in heaven and on earth is named, 16 that according to the riches of his glory he may grant you to be strength-ened with power through his Spirit in your inner being, 17 so that Christ may dwell in your hearts through faith—that you, being rooted and grounded in love, 18 may have strength to comprehend with all the saints what is the breadth and length and height and depth, 19 and to know the love of Christ that surpasses knowledge, that you may be filled with all the fullness of God.

20 Now to him who is able to do far more abundantly than all that we ask or think, according to the power at work within us, 21 to him be glory in the church and in Christ Jesus throughout all generations, forever and ever. Amen.

4 I therefore, a prisoner for the Lord, urge you to walk in a manner worthy of the calling to which you have been called, 2 with all humility and gentleness, with patience, bearing with one another in love, 3 eager to maintain the unity of the Spirit in the bond of peace. 4 There is one body and one Spirit—just as you were called to the one hope that belongs to your call— 5 one Lord, one faith, one baptism, 6 one God and Father of all, who is over all and through all and in all. 7 But grace was given to each one of us according to the measure of Christ's gift.
8 Therefore it says,

"When he ascended on high he led a host of captives,

   and he gave gifts to men."

9 (In saying, "He ascended," what does it mean but that he had also descended into the lower regions, the earth? 10 He who descended is the one who also ascended far above all the heavens, that he might fill all things.) 11 And he gave the apostles, the prophets, the evangelists, the shepherds and teachers, 12 to equip the saints for the work of ministry, for building up the body of Christ, 13 until we all attain to the unity of the faith and of the knowledge of the Son of God, to mature manhood, to the measure of the stature of the fullness of Christ, you, along with all malice.

14 so that we may no longer be children, tossed to and fro by the waves and carried about by every wind of doctrine, by human cunning, by craftiness in deceitful schemes. 15 Rather, speaking the truth in love, we are to grow up in every way into him who is the head, into Christ, 16 from whom the whole body, joined and held together by every joint with which it is equipped, when each part is working properly, makes the body grow so that it builds itself up in love.

The New Life

17 Now this I say and testify in the Lord, that you must no longer walk as the Gentiles do, in the futility of their minds. 18 They are darkened in their understanding, alienated from the life of God because of the ignorance that is in them, due to their hardness of heart. 19 They have become callous and have given themselves up to sensuality, greedy to practice every kind of impurity. 20 But that is not the way you learned Christ!— 21 assuming that you have heard

about him and were taught in him, as the truth is in Jesus, 22 to put off your old self, which belongs to your former manner of life and is corrupt through deceitful desires, 23 and to be renewed in the spirit of your minds, 24 and to put on the new self, created after the likeness of God in true righteousness and holiness.

25 Therefore, having put away falsehood, let each one of you speak the truth with his neighbor, for we are members one of another. 26 Be angry and do not sin; do not let the sun go down on your anger, 27 and give no opportunity to the devil. 28 Let the thief no longer steal, but rather let him labor, doing honest work with his own hands, so that he may have something to share with anyone in need.

29 Let no corrupting talk come out of your mouths, but only such as is good for building up, as fits the occasion, that it may give grace to those who hear. 30 And do not grieve the Holy Spirit of God, by whom you were sealed for the day of redemption. 31 Let all bitterness and wrath and anger and clamor and slander be put away from you, along with all malice. 32 Be kind to one another, tenderhearted, forgiving one another, as God in Christ forgave you.

5 Therefore be imitators of God, as beloved children. 2 And walk in love, as Christ loved us and gave himself up for us, a fragrant offering and sacrifice to God.

3 But sexual immorality and all impurity or covetousness must not even be named among you, as is proper among saints. 4 Let there be no filthiness nor foolish talk nor crude joking, which are out of place, but instead let there be thanksgiving. 5 For you may be sure of this, that everyone who is sexually immoral or impure, or who is covetous (that is, an idolater), has no inheritance in the kingdom of Christ and God. 6 Let no one deceive you with empty words, for because of these things the wrath of God comes upon the sons of disobedience. 7 Therefore do not become partners with them; 8 for at one time you were darkness, but now you are light in the Lord. Walk as children of light 9 (for the fruit of light is found in all that is good and right and true), 10 and try to discern what is pleasing to the Lord. 11 Take no part in the unfruitful works of darkness, but instead expose them. 12 For it is shameful even to speak of the things that they do in secret. 13 But when anything is exposed by the light, it becomes visible, 14 for anything that becomes visible is light. Therefore it says,

"Awake, O sleeper,

    and arise from the dead,

and Christ will shine on you."

15 Look carefully then how you walk, not as unwise but as wise, 16 making the best use of the time, because the days are evil. 17 Therefore do not be foolish, but understand what the will of the Lord is. 18 And do not get drunk with wine, for that is debauchery, but be filled with the Spirit, 19 addressing one another in psalms and hymns and spiritual songs, singing and making melody to the Lord with your heart, 20 giving thanks always and for everything to God the Father in the name of our Lord Jesus Christ, 21 submitting to one another out of reverence for Christ.

22 Wives, submit to your own husbands, as to the Lord. 23 For the husband is the head of the wife even as Christ is the head of the church, his body, and is himself its Savior. 24 Now as the church submits to Christ, so also wives should submit in everything to their husbands.

25 Husbands, love your wives, as Christ loved the church and gave himself up for her, 26 that he might sanctify her, having cleansed her by the washing of water with the word, 27 so that he might present the church to himself in splendor, without spot or wrinkle or any such thing, that she might be holy and without blemish. 28 In the same way husbands should love their wives as their own bodies. He who loves his wife loves himself. 29 For no one ever hated his own flesh, but nourishes and cherishes it, just as Christ does the church, 30 because we are members of his body. 31 "Therefore a man shall leave his father and mother and hold fast to his wife, and the two shall become one flesh." 32 This mystery is profound, and I am saying that it refers to Christ and the church. 33 However, let each one of you love his wife as himself, and let the wife see that she respects her husband.

6 Children, obey your parents in the Lord, for this is right. 2 "Honor your father and mother" (this is the first commandment with a promise), 3 "that it may go well with you and that you may live long in the land." 4 Fathers, do not provoke your children to anger, but bring them up in the discipline and instruction of the Lord.

5 Bondservants, obey your earthly masters with fear and trembling, with a sincere heart, as you would Christ, 6 not by the way of eye-service, as people-pleasers, but as bondservants of Christ, doing the will of God from the heart, 7 rendering service with a good will as to the Lord and not to man, 8 knowing that whatever good anyone does, this he will receive back from the Lord, whether he is a bondservant or is free. 9 Masters, do the same to them, and stop your threatening, knowing that he who is both their Master and yours is in heaven, and that there is no partiality with him.

10 Finally, be strong in the Lord and in the strength of his might. 11 Put on the whole armor of God, that you may be able to stand against the schemes of the devil. 12 For we do not wrestle against flesh and blood, but against the rulers, against the authorities, against the cosmic powers over this present darkness, against the spiritual forces of evil in the heavenly places. 13 Therefore take up the whole armor of God, that you may be able to withstand in the evil day, and having done all, to stand firm. 14 Stand therefore, having fastened on the belt of truth, and having put on the breastplate of righteousness, 15 and, as shoes for your feet, having put on the readiness given by the gospel of peace.

16 In all circumstances take up the shield of faith, with which you can extinguish all the flaming darts of the evil one; 17 and take the helmet of salvation, and the sword of the Spirit, which is the word of God, 18 praying at all times in the Spirit, with all prayer and supplication. To that end, keep alert with all perseverance, making supplication for all the saints, 19 and also for me, that words may be given to me in opening my mouth boldly to proclaim the mystery of the gospel, 20 for which I am an ambassador in chains, that I may declare it boldly, as I ought to speak.

21 So that you also may know how I am and what I am doing, Tychicus the beloved brother and faithful minister in the Lord will tell you everything. 22 I have sent him to you for this very purpose, that you may know how we are, and that he may encourage your hearts.

23 Peace be to the brothers, and love with faith, from God the Father and the Lord Jesus Christ. 24 Grace be with all who love our Lord Jesus Christ with love incorruptible.